# NOW YOU CARE

# Now You Care

Di Brandt

Coach House Books

First edition

Published with the assistance of the Canada Council for the Arts and the
Ontario Arts Council

NATIONAL LIBRARY OF CANADA CATALOGUING IN PUBLICATION

Brandt, Di
        Now you care / Di Brandt.

Poems.

ISBN 1-55245-127-5

        I. Title.

PS8553.R2953N69 2003          C811'.54          C2003-904402-5

*for Walter*

*For the dawn, disgrace is the day to come; for the twilight the night which engulfs it. Formerly there were people of the dawn. Here we are, perhaps, at this hour of nightfall. But why crested like larks?*

– René Char

ZONE

*I was mixing stars and sand*
*In front of him*
*But he couldn't understand*
*I was keeping the lightning of*
*The thunder in my purse*
*Just in front of him*
*But he couldn't understand*
*And I had been killed a thousand times*
*Right at his feet*
*But he hadn't understood*

*– Sarain Stump*

# Zone: <le Détroit>

*after Stan Douglas*

I

Breathing yellow air
here, at the heart of the dream
of the new world,
the bones of old horses and dead Indians
and lush virgin land, dripping with fruit
and the promise of wheat,
overlaid with glass and steel
and the dream of speed:
all these our bodies
crushed to appease
the 400 & 1 gods
of the Superhighway,
NAFTA, we worship you,
hallowed be your name,
here, where we are scattered
like dust or rain in ditches,
the ghosts of passenger pigeons
clouding the silver towered sky,
the future clogged in the arteries
of the potholed city,
*Tecumseh, come back to us*
*from your green grave,*
sing us your song of bravery
on the lit bridge over the black river,
splayed with grief over the loss
of its ancient rainbow coloured
fish swollen joy.
Who shall be fisher king
over this poisoned country,
whose borders have become
a mockery,
blowing the world to bits

with cars and cars and trucks and electricity and cars,
who will cover our splintered
bones with earth and blood,
who will sing us back into –

2

See how there's no one going to Windsor,
only everyone coming from?
Maybe they've been evacuated,
maybe there's nuclear war,
maybe when we get there we'll be the only ones.
See all those trucks coming toward us,
why else would there be rush hour on the 401
on a Thursday at nine o'clock in the evening?
I counted 200 trucks and 300 cars
and that's just since London.
See that strange light in the sky over Detroit,
see how dark it is over Windsor?
You know how people keep disappearing,
you know all those babies born with deformities,
you know how organ thieves follow tourists
on the highway and grab them at night
on the motel turnoffs,
you know they're staging those big highway accidents
to increase the number of organ donors?
My brother knew one of the guys paid to do it,
$100,000 for twenty bodies
but only if the livers are good.
See that car that's been following us for the last hour,
see the pink glow of its headlights in the mirror?
That's how you know.
Maybe we should turn around,
maybe we should duck so they can't see us,
maybe it's too late,
maybe we're already dead,
maybe the war is over,
maybe we're the only ones alive.

3

So there I am, sniffing around
the railroad tracks
in my usual quest for a bit of wildness,
weeds, something untinkered with,
goldenrod, purple aster, burdocks,
defiant against creosote,
my prairie blood surging
in recognition and fellow feeling,
and O god, missing my dog,
and hey, what do you know,
there's treasure here
among these forgotten weeds,
so this is where they hang out,
all those women's breasts
cut off to keep our lawns green
and dandelion free,
here they are, dancing
their breastly ghost dance,
stirring up a slight wind in fact
and behaving for all the world
like dandelions in seed,
their featherwinged purple nipples
oozing sticky milk,
so what am I supposed to do,
pretend I haven't seen them
or like I don't care
about all these missing breasts,
how they just vanish
from our aching chests
and no one says a word,
and we just strap on fake ones
and the dandelions keep dying,
and the grass on our lawns
gets greener and greener
and greener

4

This gold and red autumn heat,
this glorious tree splendour,
splayed out for sheer pleasure
over asphalt and concrete,
ribbons of dark desire
driving us madly toward death,
perverse, presiding over
five o'clock traffic
like the queens on Church Street
grand in their carstopping
high heels and blond wigs
and blue makeup, darling,
so nice to see you, and what,
dear one, exactly was the rush?
Or oceans, vast beyond ridicule
or question, and who cares if it's
much too hot for November,
isn't it gorgeous, darling,
and even here, in this
most polluted spit of land
in Canada, with its heart
attack and cancer rates,
the trees can still knock
you out with their loveliness
so you just wanna drop
everything and weep, or laugh,
or gather up the gorgeous
leaves, falling, and throw yourself
into them like a dead man,
or a kid, or dog,

5

O the brave deeds of men!
M*E*N, that is, they with phalli
dangling from their thighs,
how they dazzle me with
their daring exploits
every time I cross the Detroit River,
from down under, I mean,
who else could have given
themselves so grandly,
obediently, to this water god,
this fierce charlatan,
this glutton for sailors and young boys,
risking limbs and lives, wordlessly,
wrestling primordial mud
so that we, mothers and maids,
could go shopping across the border
and save ourselves twenty minutes
coming and going, chatting about
this and that, our feet never
leaving the car, never mind
the mouth of the tunnel
is haunted by bits and fragments
of shattered bone and looking
every time like Diana's bridge
in Paris, this is really grand, isn't it,
riding our cars under the river
and coming out the other side
illegal aliens, needing passports,
and feeling like we accomplished
something, snatched from
our busy lives, just being there

# Afterworlds

Gwendolyn, I call you back
    from your bed of roots, delicious
        under moist scented worm nudged earth,
speak to me,
    rising from my bed of stone,
        finding the courtyard empty,
the gate swinging open,

    O prophetess of blood and fire,
        your famous ancient lions crouched
beside Lake Ontario,
    drunk on the jewelled wine of death,

        tell me, in this unexpected resurrection,
as from drowned Atlantis out of the carnelian sea,
    as from the sister watching the sister
        who lies down
on the long stemmed wet grass under
    rumbling steel bridges,

        grateful after everything for he
who childishly plucked out her eye,
    blinding her into buffalo hoofed sage scented
        seeing,
tell me, princess of Babylon,
    what would you have said,

        had you been able, in that last moment
before the animal darkness,
    to speak,
        your brutal jewels flashing ornate in the naked
prairie sun,
    and in what tongue, outliving for one flaming second
        the devastating stages of your catastrophic
loves,

tell me, Gwendolyn,
        how should I find my way
among these empty incantations,
    these chipped white dishes on soap sudded oilcloth,
        these nothing signs
among the walking dead,
    the lilies sprouting tiger lips and rust,


        the prairie struggling to remember
its dream wild partridge feathered feast, that exuberant
    drumming?

# Castle walk

*after Alain Robbe-Grillet*

Curses on she who asked to be
ordinary
among painted plates and cups
and bits of jam left on spoons,
willing to forget
fire flashing through
silver sheeted clouds,
her forehead bleeding,
her ragged torn heart.

❦

*In prison we ate rats*
*after drying them in the sun.*
*Every night God visited us*
*in our cells,*
*soothing or frightening us*
*with his velvet hands*
*and invisible dark sword.*

❦

Even now I could leap
off any shining parapet
at high noon
into the Devil's arms
in search of that fire,
were it not for the garden warbler
nesting in the rhododendron,
pink and scarlet blossomed
under the Castle Walk,
the bluebells blazing
beside the sycamore.

�֎

The water at the bottom
of the well
remembers Queen Victoria,
Sir Wallace, and the numbers
of the dead.
Here in this red rock
overhanging the sweet path
tremble the memories
of cave dwellers,
shuddering their easy
ecstasy.

✶

I cannot compute it.
Even on the windiest days,
the chorus of ancestors
full throated among the trees,
bits of severed limbs
float through the room,
the blue plastic thermos
in the window promises
black tea and landmines
halfway across the world.
The surface keeps slipping, Alain.
Somewhere deep inside us
the centre holds.
Say it is so, Chinua,
say it is so.

# The poets visit the Rosewell Arms

Surprised to find,
on their country rambles,
how he singles her out
in every pub,
the 'village drunk,'
proclaiming his love:

*They don't know, Robbie,*
*they don't know,*
*the kinship of those*
*who walk,*
*as we have done,*
*through living fire.*

His friends clap him
on the back, laugh,
pour him another drink,
she turns back to the bar,
smiling, glass in hand,
discussing Yeats.

The floor rocks under
his sea legs, his skin burns.
Long ago he learned
to substitute drink
for touch, to hold
the terror in.

*So many unrequited*
*singers, Bobby.*
*The fire made diamonds*
*of your eyes.*
*The breathing world cries,*
*'I love you too.'*

# A modest proposal

This night I am haunted by your stray dogs, Frankie,
of Albert Street, their thin, eager love, abject,

you called it, useful, waving your hand, smiling slightly, over
shrimp cocktail and Chablis, nicely

chilled, their backbones broken, flesh frozen into fear.
Let me confess, dear Francis, your confessions were not

unattractive to me, your wife the psychologist busy
helping every poor sinner and no time for you.

Your shaking hand, your heaving trembling chest.
Your twenty year sacrifice of every tender feeling

in the name of civic love. Your soldier's fortitude.
Your impressive million dollar contract to inject them

with whatever poison you feel like to advance our knowledge
of their pain. Like every poet I can

assure you I have prostituted myself for less, gathering fuel
in vacant lots, *so zu sprechen, Herr Doktor,*

wagging my tail eagerly, panting for healing in the morning
and vivisection at night, suffering

my sainthood graciously, my bowels domesticated,
my howls unheard in the abandoned hermitage.

## St. Norbert in August

How the primroses hurt us
in the ripeness of summer
among the cathedral ruins,
the stones singing,
the grass stirring in the heat,
bees thrumming,
the flies lazy, contented,
the shining wheat
('O how the wheat is shining')
the brown river sluggish,
the gnarled apple trees,
the maples surrounded by light,
the goldenrod,
the grasshoppers,
sweet clover on the wind,
wild turkeys parading
through the wild grass,
the sun heavy on the earth,
our thirsty skin heaving,
the bandura dancing, O!

# St. Norbert in July

*after Louise Halfe*

Throb of buffalo
herds, drumming
under the earth.
Whiff of sage
in the wind.
Chokecherry
branches, bowing,
heavy with fruit.
Sob of grass.
Wheels rumbling.
Burning tipis,
smoking flesh.
I Thirst Dance,
Ghost Dance,
I Give-Away Dance,
Beg Dance.
'Shot our children
as they gathered
wood.'

Skull Dance.
'A mountain of bones.'

# Accidentally

Because the millennium has ended. Because the children have taken over the monasteries, and filled them with fishnets, wildflowers, paper lanterns, donkeys made of straw.

Because Our Lady of the Prairies stepped down off her pedestal last August, walked across the yellow stubble fields in her white silk dress, and didn't come back.

When the rivers flooded and the grass along the banks turned black, and the mosquitoes came, billions of them, to plague us.

Our first born, daughters, angry as hell at our parental betrayal of them, we didn't know, we didn't know.

At the poetry festival, all the young women wore violets and goldenrod in their hair.

They said the house was haunted, and it was, the dead walking through it, dazed, in black and red velvet, the children screaming at them, joyful and afraid, the monks sullen, retreating in the shadows.

Alissa, alone among the children, stared back at the ghost bride in her faded brocade, let the white gloved hand of death touch her cheek, and didn't flinch. Her memory welling up in her like a flame, spider knowledge.

You were there, then, with red hair, carrying one of the dead over your shoulder, and your aura of sadness, in all that commotion, cut a wave of silence in the air.

Who knows why anything happens? Or how lucky we are, in spite of these alarms, these signs of an era ending, and new beginnings?

The spirits have been good to us, have visited us, with blessings, in spite of our inattention, our distractedness, and yes, we are grateful, we are deeply grateful, though we have forgotten the words for this prayer, this alleluia, this amen.

# Dog days in Maribor
## Anti (electric) ghazals

I

Truly, in this age,
why should not all women be mad?

The snapping turtle stares
at the giant ball of rope in the sky.

The cherry trees have all been cut;
bronzed epitaphs.

No more invasions!
The earth is spitting up blood.

Diamond rivers, uranium valleys,
petroleum oceans.

Purple irises, Van Gogh, radiant,
beside the door.

2

These days it is the dogs, gold hearted,
who must teach us.

We are spinning in space
in the key of C# minor.

Or spiders, dizzy, drunk,
flying out over the river Esk.

Who shall console us,
with the belly dancers on strike?

These celestial vanishings,
these drowned continents,

the lightning fields flashing
all night long in the rain.

3

Whose grief is this, wild haired,
singing, in the wind?

Chokecherry blossoms,
canker worms, rustling prairie grass.

The gorgeous eye of the dead deer,
iridescent, terrible.

In the desert I heard
stones weeping.

Every breath, every pulse,
every shiver rippling out, forever.

In every cave a gypsy.
Our embroidered dead, O beloved.

4

These dozen hooded faces
empty, hollow, turned to the sun.

Arthritic symptoms
could mean: mineral deficiencies,

deer ticks, genetic weaknesses,
accumulated steroids,

unexpressed rage.
So many empty gin bottles

behind the red woodshed.
So much depends upon.

Signs and wonders,
*earth grommets* in the fields.

5

Shall we harness the stones,
verily, bind them with steel?

The blackbirds are angry:
give them back their seeds.

We who have lived without
hope, these long centuries,

can we survive one more winter?
Mice huddled in tree roots,

hawk's shadow.
Goose down, bilberries,

hot lava. Brandy
in small glasses, *na zdravje.*

6

Tell the doctors:
no more chemotherapies!

All our rivers and lakes now glow
in the dark.

sk8 duking it out with the partisans,
Darth Vader spidering

through the medieval town square
of pink roofed Maribor.

Trout leaping from the river Drava
into the fishermen's hands.

Blond boys, insistent: so many
innocent ex-communists to exploit.

7

What was it we wanted,
before all the walls came down?

Blue grey eyes, looking at me,
through the cigarette smoke.

*Heil Mister Herr Direktor Daddy*
*Doktor Präsident CEO Sir!*

That is no country for old women,
every oak slashed from root to crown.

The children breathing in
the by-products of petroleum.

Vineyards gleaming,
fruitladen, on the sun drenched hills.

8

Let us have more mastectomies,
cut them all off!

Once out of nature we can sing
all the louder, n'est-ce pas,

ma soeur, mon semblable?
The disobedient cells vanquished,

a clean nation without breasts,
once and for all.

Flat-chested mothers renouncing
their children in the public baths.

The poets ranting beautifully
in the dark, drunk on stolen wine.

9

So many newly minted young
capitalists on the make.

The golden rule:
self sacrifice, or suicide.

The curve of the sweet earth,
herb scented, holy.

Bring them along, these crotch sniffers,
these bags of fur,

squirrel chasers, diggers of corpses,
rollers in horse dung.

Rotted fish on the world's beaches,
jewelled with black flies, beetles.

10

Now that it's much much too late,
now you care.

Poison ivy wrapped around the
ash trees; lover's embrace.

Turtle, are you crazy, get
your diamond shell off the damn road.

The eating and the eaten, all
are gathered here, dearly beloved.

The blood, the liver, remember
our mother tongues.

A species gone every three minutes.
History racing us by.

11

Thank you Chrysler for this squashed
gopher blood bug feast amen.

I touch the earth, the earth touches me.
I feel the earth, the earth feels me.

Twenty-five billion Barbies,
plastic harems for everyone.

The yard hungry for rust, seducing
dead cars in the rain.

Each of us flaunting our
skeletons in front of the Opera Café,

elbows flying, eyes in the trees.
Fire-fangled feathers dangling down.

Crowds pacing at the entrances
to the realms of the dead.

Thing One and Thing Two
in boots and black leather:

It was you, no it was you.
You you you you you you you.

Dancing under red electric light
to Mozart's *Requiem*.

How much did you have to bribe
the ferryman?

Guarding the gate for your beloveds.
Well, what would you do?

# Tally

*for Anna*

Knowing before knowing, the grey gnaw in the bone.

The dark: a gorgeous woman lifting her skirt.

Seeing the boat crash seconds before the boat crashed
in the river. Six drowned bodies under the bridge.

*Not enuff goddamn love.*

If this was karma I can tell you a huge helluva debt.
Five million heartbreaks. See, the scars on my belly.

A graceful way out, legal, medicalized, nurses carrying trays. Drugs.
Grateful. Amnesia.

Too many bloody people in the world anyway, cancer
of the earth.

The soldiers in the forest. The neglectful father. You.

Kayak on still water, ineffable. Laughter of women,
silver fluted.

Sweating through the land claims file, line by line.
The people versus the corporation. Trees and fish
versus pulp and paper.

Your dead mother beckons in moonlight over the
black lake, come, come.

Rootprints. The implacable hand of the Law.

Birdsong at daybreak. Wet muzzle of dog. Seder with candlelight.
Montreal bagels.

Not yet. Beloved.

# The poets reflect on their craft

Some days like pulling teeth, rotten roots.
Staring down the barrel of the gun.
Shooting the town clock.
Forty days in the desert.
Fifty days in the desert, no food and water.
The devil sticking out his tongue.
Electric shock. Thunderbolt.
Heroin. Poison in the veins.
Angels beating their wings on your bared skull.
Who will believe you.
Moon in your hands, transparent, luminous.
Cursed by God.
Cursed by mothers, fathers, brothers, the bloody town hall.
Bereft.
Dogs limping on three paws.
The fourth one sawed off by a car wheel, careening.
The devil making faces.
Long red tongue, goats' horns, trampling the streets of Ptuj,
announcing spring.
Licking licking. Cunt or wound.
Bad gas leaking from stones, earth fissures.
Nettles. Poison ivy. Bee sting.
Rotgut. Fungus on your toes.
Wild strawberries low to the ground, cheating the lawn mower.
A wall waiting for the wrecker's ball.
Clear vodka. Ice.

# Forest slippers

*after Maymee Ying Lum*

At night the bed becomes a boat, and the grandmothers rise
up out of the sea, white hair streaming in the wind. They giggle
too much, the emperor decided, I must teach them reason, so he
ordered his guards to cut off the head of his favourite, clenching
his fists at night against his fierce loss. Clutching her hybrid
identities, she collects small discarded objects and ties them with
bits of coloured silk and arranges them in neat whimsical rows.
Under the yellowing prairie grass, she hears faint drumming of
buffalo hooves, sharp hunters' cries, thud of bodies hitting earth.
Despite their fervent prayers they couldn't stop the railway from
destroying their solitude, so they retreated inland, abandoning
their beloved gardens and shy fourlegged friends. You must go,
you must go immediately, the monks said, full of panic, motioning
to mom and grandma, waiting for grandpa in the car at the end
of the long driveway, but grandpa had taken the keys with him,
so they sat there, giggling nervously, while the monks scurried
anxiously to their rooms. Here I will build my dream, she whispers,
on the edge of this forest, drummers and poets and aliens meeting
under the night sky, trace of coyotes among these standing stones.
Let us find out then, said the king, where these princesses go at
night to wear out their dancing shoes by morning. And those are
pearls, and these their mutilated broken feet, and these the tears
that were their eyes. We are much too far out at sea for such a
little wooden box, says the eldest sister, if we concentrate, perhaps
we can fly. Sing me home, the nimble footed raven haired Metis
lover croons, before I die. Pistol shots, hail Mary full of grace,
storks and eagles circling, scent of white chrysanthemums, wild
mint and sage.

# Wake up

## Four quartets

I

Tangle of wild tansy
in every crack,
old rag and bone shop
left open to rain.

Clear high notes
piercing the sky.

Like weeds, grandma said.
The knife edge of pleasure
blitzed by love, O!

Underground rivers,
diamonds, leaf mould.

Impossibly, and yet
this hundred-year-old wood
held through all kinds
of stormy weather.

Enough room for ghosts,
ancestral promises
breaking open.
Heap of wooden boards
in a field.

2

And why,
after so much light
through rainstreaked cloud,
this black,
this otherworldly
glimmering?

Live embers in the belly,
throat a fountain,
moon rocks in our eyes.

We were speaking
of our mothers giving
themselves so strangely
away, imprudent.

Argument of sisters:
let her go, yes, no, yes, no.

Her empty fridge,
her long life.

Wild scented meadow,
grasshopper sung,
sun drenched,
holding us earthbound.

In love with grass,
and wonder.

3

These uninvited, insistent,
haunting us to the grave
if necessary, to be noticed.

These sisters and cousins,
who will not escape
the leaking boat,
careening crazily toward
rock and quicksand,
will not remember
the killing games
in grandpa's yard.

These friends,
who played along carefully,
watching their backs, turning
as the wind turns,
remember precisely
nothing.

And there's no way
to love or leave them
here at this breaking shore!

Transparencies, pink dawn
above the trees,
poetry of birds,
symphonic,
country matters ...

Face nestled in goose down,
not yet, not yet.

4

The molten core heaves
burning rocks into the air.

Jester, fire eater, dance, dance,
juggle on your pyramid of sticks.

And here, and here, and here,
these animal calligraphies
every child can read.

Every moth, every bee,
the fallen tree, leaf covered,
tender red earth.

Trailing meteor dust
we come falling down.

Toes nudging the cliff edge
scan the great dark,
diamond laced, roiling –

Ether swirling, every molecule
shattering into space.

Handful of asteroid dust.

Leap into nothing, joyful,
let them weep.

# Interspecies communication

*for Aganetha Dyck and the bees*

And then everything goes bee,
sun exploding into green,
the mad sky dive
through shards of diamond light,
earth veering left, then right,
then left, sweet scented,
the honing in,
the buzz,
the yes no dance,
the quantum leap into
open swoon of calendula,
yellow orange delphinium starflower,
ultraviolet milkweed forget-me-not,
caress of corolla carpel calyx,
sharp tongue flick into nectar,
delicious rub of belly against silk,
shudder of pollenheavy thighs,
the long slow sip of honeymead,
sigh of sated petals in the wind,
the drunken stagger hiveward,
confused weave through
chlorpyrifos malathion,
ribboned corridors of poisoned
insectless late afternoon air,
*drumbee doombledore hummabee*
the familiar brush swarm crawl
of bee on bee on bee on bee,
sentries,
warriors,
scouts,
promiscuous,
architects,
sculptors,
whimsical,
perfectionist,

singers,
nurses,
studs,
this honeyed home,
*Tech Midchuarta,*
this droning harem,
this 'feminine monarchie,'
the mother deep in her dark cell,
quivering licked and adored,
O mother bride,
O queen of earth and sky,
O goddess
at the end of this dark century
of human destruction
and despair,
as always of joyful, delirious
magick flowered
honey love

# Songs for a divorce

*Who shall revoke jubilance?*

*– Rainer Maria Rilke*

I

Reaching round
the brick walls
at last,
we found
ashes and raging
hot flame

It was too late then,
dear heart,
wasn't it,
though we cried
and tried,
furiously,
for many furious
months,
to save
the smoking wreckage

(heroically,
not thinking of
ourselves)

2

though I'm
puzzled now
to contemplate

breakfast plates
thrown across
kitchens and
doors slammed,
and windows,
old, bevelled,
the original
irreplaceable glass,
smashed

as a method
to save anything,
let alone
everything

3

Loving each other
beautifully
we thought
would, grandly
and single-
handedly,
take on

our unreasonable fathers,
our helpless mothers,
the war,
the Capitalist System,
environmental pollution,

and save us from
boredom,
suffocation,
indignation,
and mediocre economic destinies

4

You sang me,
O husband of forests
and beaches,

with your eyes,
and lips,
and hands,

bright coloured
canvasses,
your unreasonable joy,

your castles of sticks
in sand,

irreverent
jester's bells,

airplane tickets,
dreamer,

into life

5

At night I lay
naked
in your dark arms,

naked

6

Forgive me, beloved,
for loving
the hero I made
of you,

cradling your
knife wounds
as children

7

When I think
about it:
nearly killing
each other

for love.

8

How could we
have known,

    lost children
floundering,
with the flimsiest
of life jackets,

    in that cold sea?

9

*She walks these hills*
*in a long dark veil,*
*She visits my grave*
*when the dark winds wail.*


I love you, I love you not.

I told you once,
but you forgot.

10

Our dark bellies
opening

    in each other's faces, spinning

to black

       space

II

keeping *forever* lit,
shining,
through regret

disguised as border hostilities, war

12

Whatever there is in me
that is singing,
whatever there is in me,


you are there too

# Portrait of the artist as a young hero

I see him poised like a dancer
on his lithe feet.
He is fifteen, the ground opens
under him:
    ready to leap –

The house swirls around him,
silver vortices of rage,
helpless
unnameable griefs.

The dinner table teeters
in their midst,
    a ship at sea.

The stepmother's rules,
no doubt about it, are
efficient and clear
and have brought a sort
    of order
to this floundering house,
with its half dozen
unruly
motherless
growing boys.

If parsimonious.
If lacking in joy, or love, or play.
If grim.

'Only one kind of spread
on your bread.'

Your fifteen-year-old father
grins, his dark brown eyes
    dancing,

an uncanny likeness of
his dead mother.

Everyone watching,
he slowly, dramatically,
spreads peanut butter
on the bottom half,
    the 'skirt.'

Silence.
Pass the jam, please.

More slowly, Picassoesque,
he sculpts
red strawberry jam
in two impressive whorls,
on the top,
    the 'blouse.'

Little Timmy whimpers,
sensing a storm.

Your young father casually
folds the bread over,
takes a bite.

Even before the deed is done,
the father,
seeing his dead wife's
loved face
whom he worshipped
but could not own,
resurrected
in the face of this
impertinent prodigal son,
who refuses

to accept the new
reasonable dispensation,
insisting on tearing open
his numb, dumb flesh,
over and over, clawing at every old
inadequacy, every wound,
goes blind
with suppressed fury.

I think of your father
dancing,
over the chasm
of his father's brass belt buckled
wrath

lightly, shielding
his head
with his arms,

then grabbing the leather,
his heart
splintering into a thousand silvered
     shards,

facing the father down.

# Dreamsongs for Eden

Dear one, I saw you
riding the wind
under a blue blue sky,
here are some black days
ahead for you.
Look! the tear in your red heart
reflects diamond shaped
shadows on the bright grass,
your spirit
among the leaping crickets,
hide it hide it!
under a grey stone.

Someday the Silver Lady
will come for you
with starry hair
and a bowl of light.
Watch for her, she carries
the moon in her belly,
she will strike you blind,
she will lift you
above clouds
to swirling galaxies.

The dogs are sprouting
extra heads and howling
under the bridges.
The bones of the drowned
children have washed down
the swollen red river.
The strewn rose petals
have shrivelled to dust.
Watch out! watch out!
Here is a long darkness
before she will save you.

Fields of stubble
lying golden, blasted by sun
after the wheat harvest.
Late August prairie soil
baked, cracked by heat.
Mama, mama,
the geese in the field
are tired
thinking of winter,
the long flight home.
The twisted golden rope
under oil slicks
drags their broken
wings down.

✗

Dear one, what have they
done to you,
your golden head
rolling in the sand?
Where are your arms
and legs now,
your round belly?
Your eyes have grown
big and luminous,
your eloquent mouth
silent.
The ones who suffer,
the ones who suffer,
lie mutilated,
washed up on beaches,
these words I sing
for you,
cracked, shivering,
vibrating
in smog.

He took you to the top
of the windswept bare hill
and looked around.
There was silence around him.
He thought it was only air.
The binding took only a minute.
You thought it was rope
for the new swing in the park.
Pierced your feet
with his awl.
Piercer, pricker, bodkin.
And packing up
quickly, suddenly afraid,
left you there.

Eden, Eden,
you still have your eyes.
Look at the sky.
The ravens gathered
in the gnarled apple tree.
They have come
to cry for you,
with raucous tongues,
their black wings flapping.

꙰

How will you walk now
with your swollen feet,
how will you live
with your swollen heart,
river of grief
overflowing
your thin veins
into grass,
the cricket sung fields,
the goldenrod,
the wild roses.

꙳

You who will grow up
without monarch butterflies
or salmon or wild bees,
for whom
cicadas and fireflies
will be quaint
electronic myths,
whose children will know
the words allergy,
asthma, panic disorder,
more intimately than
roses or celestial or sea

Do not forgive us
for worshipping death,
for crippling you
with terror,
Eden, little grandmother,
keeper of our hope.
The grief of earth
gasps
exhausted
under cement,
our great failure,
our open wound.

Is this love,
this twisted clogged
river of molten gold,
choking in chemical
saturated clay?

How he tossed you
lightly in the air once
and caught three year old
you, laughing
among the leaping
leopards and crows.
O he was the lover then,
bowing before your
golden haired childish wild joy.

Even now
he hearkens after you
beneath cocked guns.
Listen, you can hear
a heart sobbing
through cracked
grey cement.

Go to the corner
of the yard at midnight
where the grass grows
against the fence
under the crabapple tree
untouched by the lawn mower.
There she will greet you.
She has saved your broken heart
in her cupped hands,
silver red shards.
There she will pour
your spirit
like music
back into you.

In rippled sun drenched sand
I will wait for you.
There I will gather
dates for you and wash
your pierced feet
under palms.
Eden, dear one,
your sutured heart,
your curls swept by wind.

# Horizon on fire

*after René Char*

It is raining from the smokestacks on Isobel Street. The
mosquitoes are laughing, having outwitted the city yet again.
Grass between the cement blocks of the sidewalk: grin of
the wild.

❊

Even the dogs have shuddered, throwing their lot in with
humans.

❊

Fireflies, nocturnal promise.

❊

Let us now gird up our chests and loins to embrace our chagrin.

❊

The poems came in like ants, clamouring. They went out like
dancing girls. Devils and angels cheering.

❊

Should we agree the purple loosestrife along the river is beautiful
and benign, intending only to shine? Choking out even the
bulrushes, pharaoh of weeds.

❊

This is a war we don't want to win: depleted uranium, DDT,
pummelling the earth.

꙳

The grasshopper endures, prophetic, sharpening its razor song.

꙳

The whole language suffering amnesia. Glottal Alzheimer's.
Chemical cocktails in our brains.

꙳

Night and day, season after season, the predatory universe
exercises its tender heart: eating and being eaten, each with its
particular grace. The beaver becoming pond, the field mouse
becoming sky.

꙳

Tractor tracks through the shorn wheatfields. PCBs in the river.

꙳

The impossible arc of the poem, from west to east.

꙳

Born to mothers, dying to sons.

꙳

Every furled fetal frond expecting joy.

꙳

On the beach, the children scooped the dead fish out of the lake
and buried them two at a time in the sand, for love. Singing their
silent funeral song.

❊

Oil spill all over the car engine (river, ocean), every molecule vibrating, ready to burst into flame.

❊

No floor, no ceiling outside the castle (factory, prison) walls. Imagine.

❊

Even the worms must eat; yeast in our bellies.

❊

After seven centuries, the ancient Egyptian curse is lifted. See the ancestors crowding in, moths fluttering against the windshield, to have a look.

❊

What a gift it was to meet you. A chance encounter that changed the world.

❊

When did the vector leading to this moment, this lightning flash, begin?

❊

Too many deaths waiting to happen. Pick one.

❊

Those who do not look back to measure the altitude. So far above sea level. Anointed by clouds.

꙳

Singing so soon after hard rain: grass and birds spectacular in their resilience.

꙳

Your hands filled with wild strawberries (rare), pouring them into the bowl. Slanting sunlight. Stained blessing.

꙳

Just a fraction of the possible is so much more than enough.

꙳

These flashes of light in the sky, who knows their source or destination? Plucked like notes from a lyre, invisibly?

꙳

Each of us in our solitary rooms, tilting at corporations.

꙳

Let the prairie (steppe, veldt) recover its grandmotherly strength: long rooted grasses, sweet weeds.

꙳

The hum of the earth, turning. Listen. Trepidation of the spheres, a slight wobble.

꙳

At the top of the mountain, the hang-gliders, rainbow coloured, lie limp on the grass, waiting for wind. Striped dragonflies darting, collecting their morning feast.

꙰

At the end of the sweet path, where forest meets highway, these small crushed bodies.

꙰

Dusky sundown, rose coloured, petroleum tinted.

# Which side of the ocean

All these centuries
    I have missed you, Mother.
        See the gulls and loons,
crying after me.

  *Jetzt sind wir für*
      *immer unheimlich,*
trampling foreign land.

  How many bodies,
    O Misshepezhieu,
to placate
  the angry waters?

# Exhibition notes

### The Castle and the Winding Path

Great-great-grandchildren of evicted squatters etching poems
into the flagstones. Leather boots. Spiked green hair. Nails.
Glass. Rope. Composition for ten thousand loudspeakers.

### Is It Really You

Sweet pang, a continent away. Harp twang.

### The Wooden Gate

Spiders swing from the corners in every room. Bees in the walls.
Rusted enamel pot filled with dirt. Prairie happily reclaims
homestead. Roof caves, bows to rain. *Parade of Wild Geese.*
Chokecherries rain from trees.

### Wind Chimes

Ceremonies for our remembered dead, iced funeral cakes on cut
glass plates.

### A Thousand Hands

Every brick, every stone, tree, bears witness. Lichen under the
fingernails. But we, are we any different?

### The Echo in the Echo

The reappearance of the word which unfolds under the word
which revokes. Ten thousand lit candles around a pool.
Darkness.

*Allegory: Blue Satin*

The love song of the blue satin bower bird, blue pebbles, blue
satin feathers, twigs stained with wild blueberry juice, to match
her eyes.


*Except for you, what beauty?*

Lit up from within, ten thousand years of waiting flowering in
their faces, hands, feet. These our children, our wounded, our
beautiful, our singing

# HEART

*this furnace, this fire*
*in a corner of the body's dark*

*this is the place that burns*
*whatever has been broken*

— *Steven Michael Berzensky*

# Heart

And that was your mother that night,
on the dark water of Lake Winnipeg,
come, she beckoned, come, in the silver
moon's wake, and you and I dazzled
by her light and her shadowy siren song,
and you, braver and more desirous
than I, swung out onto the diamond
studded waves to greet her, and I
pulled you back onto sand, stony
arguments of earth and grass and trees,
I meant to say, but you had tasted sky,
and knew the delicate armies of the air
could enfold you against cradled
knife wounds and abandoning, and why,
you thought, and so did I, that night,
should we linger when she aches
for us too, her spirit arms lighting up
the lake, her song rippling the dark
water, the wind whispering in the reeds
behind us myriad promises

ℵ

Now that the secrets of seeing double
have been revealed, there is the luxury
of comparing landscapes, horizon lines,
the exact angle of walls, ceiling, arches
colliding, dividing, sharp lit edges, now
in focus, these two bright grey blue lakes,
two skies ringing round eternal intimations,
and I and I sliding around these surfaces,
no longer grasping for solid ground, no,
waiting rather for the noman's space
of grief and frayed nerve ends between
these severed eyes, torn limbs, shattered
heart, to embody itself, hater and hated,
embracing across these thousand
slivered lifetimes, O baby, that was
enough terror to paralyze a people,
see now you have endured, here on these
swaying shores I call you back from
horror through white bright flashes, wild
swinging across the waters, tender
rejoining, in this little upstairs room
with its infinite little windows, beloved,
to joy

*after Martín Prechtel*

Who would choose such a family, you ask,
a stone hearted mom and a dad made of fire,
imprisoning, flaying you on their Mennonite
farm like Tall Girl in her ancestral Mayan
hut? I chose a lover, like she did, who would
run away with me to sea, and was struck, like she,
by jealous lightning, and shattered, scattered
then, all over the singing fields, this is the work
of ecstasy, says Martín, cracking us open so
we can shine, and here in the cooking pot, under
our mother's contrite stone bed, I gurgle and
burble and stew, preening my scales and feathers,
as always she is too impatient, and I will be
let out too soon, and my voice will have turned
to raven's, and instead of embracing her I will fly,
toward the never before seen beautiful shining
thing, already the Sun and Moon are plotting
to live the whole story again, and we not done
weeping, the funeral meats furnishing as usual
the marriage table, and Tall Girl running down
from the mountain across the yellow prairie
with her forbidden wild secret lover, saltily,
north to the sea

᪶

These ways we can and cannot touch, and I
wanting to bring you armfuls and armfuls
of light, and shells, and bits of bone, from
this magical lake, with its whimsical, many
coloured heart shaped stones, and wild
diamonded waves' wombed cadences,
and mothers with young children, and boys
on motor bikes, insisting noisily they are men,
to stretch out the moment of our meeting,
in the room, in the house, on the street,
in the city, its proper beginning and end,
somewhere in another galaxy we are lovers
in that other way, this also is plenitude,
this spirit ride through the outer dimensions
of human space in search of my lost face,
and you there holding me against flying apart
with your wise grace, these inland seas we
carry in us, deep tides, these waves we can
ride quantumly to dream time and back,
laced with this sweet exquisite painful edge,
this other worldliness

꙰

Hummingbird whale vibrations rippling
out across the ocean sky, fast and high
and deep and low, and we, our old griefs
unfurling under the ash trees, nosing
the elements for their interspecies song,
these long aerial arcs, these wide under
water glides, earth hooting cooing her
large pleasure, north to south and south
to north, her global sonata, her Madonna
cello suite, here they come winging
diving through us, here, hold my hand
in all this space, dear friend, this open
field, fall and rise, and we mere grace notes,
small decoration to this huge symphony,
we with our thin paraphernalia, here,
under the ash trees, this sweet night,
our cement lanes and sidewalks, our
caught breaths, our pesticides, wild
pebble consciousness, blood, dreaming

'On some sophisticated taping machine he slowed down the hummingbird songs until they
were almost a set of subsonic twinklings. ... For days on end, pods upon pods of whales of
every kind came rolling in, breaching and blowing along side the ship, diving and gathering
around the underwater speakers, chattering, hooting and cooing in courteous, measured replies
between the hummingbirds' phrases. Slightly chagrined, the elated ship's research personnel
recorded the whales' exuberant conversation and after speeding them up found themselves
listening to some very ornate hummingbird songs!' Martín Prechtel, *The Disobedience of the
Daughter of the Sun: Ecstasy and Time* (Cambridge, Mass: Yellow Moon Press, 2001), 128.

✣

Trudging slowly across the pasture
in single file, chewing, flicking flies
with lazy tails, 7-Up, Coca-Cola, Orange
Crush, Betty and de Roude, named after
our neighbour Izak Feah, his car a '58
blue Chevy, no red in her anywhere,
*Na nü go*, Roude, Izak would chuckle,
slapping the steering wheel, slamming
the accelerator, whoa, Roude, he'd say,
knocked backward, stay Roude, lurching
forward, our Roude was in fact red,
nothing horsey or carlike about her,
a bland do gooder, but what about
Betty in her quiet stall, nearly invisible
among all the loud cows, neutral and mild
like our aunt Nettie, who never ever
uttered an angry word, while the others
bellowed and kicked and pissed loudly
during milking, even after our dad
started playing Mozart on the barn
radio to calm them down, preferring
Grandma's raucous hymns, Washed
in the blood, her rough cheek caressing
their hot flanks, instead

✼

Here at the heart of the ravaged heart
of the Dead Land, lilacs mixing with
the dead rain, we like to kill our gods
and eat them too, like all good christians
do, no mystery moths or beetles for us,
or locusts shining in the grass, nosiree,
all our trillion little winged deities, bees,
mosquitoes, houseflies, butterflies,
fruitflies, fishflies, horseflies, Junebugs,
cicadas now in radical chemical jeopardy,
and our lettuce and raspberries, and yet,
and yet, deer graze in the forest along
the ravine, grasshoppers and crickets
miraculously sing in forgotten ditches
along the fields, wasps stray through
chlorpyrifos clouds to out of the way
sweet milkweed, thistle, goldenrod
clumps, just then for a moment, above
around below the shadow of the shadow
of these endless depleted uranium driven
grey grey grey grey grey apocalyptic
streets, these lurking cancer cells, hawks
and goldfinches, bright coloured, let's
turn it all around, asphalt splitting
volcanic magic, blue butterflies, sweet
grass, adrenalin, circling darting
fluttering kicking bursting in

❧

*for Alexis*

That time you were dead and made of clay,
and saw from the ceiling the seam of your
cracked heart unevenly stitched and glowing
in the dark, and your friend raised you back
into this same life, this world with its
jack hammer love tearing it apart, and you
understood a continent is not big enough
for the enemies in your blood, and one half
followed your father, truant, truculent,
across the tarmac sea, the other stayed,
the moon playing on her black hair under
the quivering hibiscus at night, and you too
green to be her man, these our mothers,
their sighs, their salty washed eyes, long
hands hearkening after us on the gravel
path through the trees, their lost hope
on our lips, and we vaulting through clouds,
seeking our futures fugitively

✴

You and I and our epic heroic lives,
Alexis, huh, so far beyond what will
be said or remembered of us, riding
the wind on our flimsiest gossamer
wishes out over the concrete walls of
our abandonment, our pierced soles,
mortified karmic selves, bowing through
tall clouds to touch tender, moist earth,
amid thunder and hailing stones, the
unspeakable thing that haunts us, these
shivering creatures soaked by rain,
mad kings, weed crowned on the wild heath,
carrying Cordelia in our mutilated arms,
imagining new helmets for the invisible
legion of spirit guards, you will say they
are Persian, across the torn sky, but let
them be changed, first lightning, then
flaming sunset, fluorescent, rainbow coloured,
everything shivering, sated, lifting itself
through rough strife, aching with love,
is it not so, Alexis, into starry night

❊

Your vanilla heart, your full moon
marigold honey bear senses, your
high voltage barbed wire electric
fences, your spiked iron gates, your
automatic supersonic paranoid
antennae, my vanilla heart, my full
moon marigold honey bear senses,
my automatic supersonic paranoid
antennae, O do not ask what is it,
my high voltage barbed wire electric
fences, my spiked iron gates, three
cigarettes in an oyster shell, this
sawdust visit, mermaids, you and I,
shooting across the sky

✼

Don't laugh when I confess every cobalt
coloured little lake along the Trans-Canada
is flooding where I cried for you, hungry
tires eating the pavement from Winnipeg
to Couchiching and Shabbaqua, my body
hurtling through spruce scented air toward
polluted Ontario, my spirit reaching long
arms back across the miles to open prairie,
deer among the aspen of La Barrière Forest,
singers around a fire, your filmmaker's eye,
your poet's tongue, your quicksilver
philosopher's mind, quivering skin, naked
heart, how do you know if you're crazy,
these commuter lives, from exhausting
winters in dirty cities to snatched moments
in paradise, being with you, sunflower
mosquito dragonfly grasshopper ice in
the lungs wish it could last happiness

✗

*for Dorothy*

Look to the whales, the children said,
the indigo auraed children of Bulgaria,
and that was the summer the whales began
beaching themselves disastrously on sand,
shot out of the sea by intolerable sonar
x-rays from powerful military submarines,
that was the summer Berlin flooded, and
Cambodia, and Australia, and we understood
all our horrified anxieties may after all
come true, and there may indeed be men
in asbestos suits experimenting somewhere
in Alaska with the world's weather, and
we may not be able to turn it around, this
mad ecosuicidal embrace of death dealing
technologies in our hysterical flight from
death, our fathers leaping when they get
it from tall bridges into white water, our
sons crashing violently into steep ditches,
desperate escape into each other's elements,
thrashing through species barriers, looking
for extra spirit to unlock our clenched arms,
fear of annihilation, the soft shoed feathered
children of Bulgaria tuned to new dimensions
of indigo coloured hope

♓

The raw iron taste of blood in your mouth,
huh George, shudder of flesh against steel,
the whole world knows your secret now,
your twisted pleasure, don't it make you
hard, George, all that innocent skin torn to
scarlet bits, ribbons festooning the smoky
sky, bigger balls than your dad, huh George,
here we thought you was a little guy, all
that whiskey on the brain and your arm
easily the thickest, longest, quickest, strongest,
but aren't you ashamed, George, waving it
around like that, or at least nervous, ain't
you heard, the killer bees in this desert is
attracted to missile honey, all that sexy
crumpled depleted uranium to caress,
O, O, O, George, you shouldn't have,
you shouldn't have, you shouldn't have

If I could end this war before it's begun
by laying my life down in bloody Washington,
I would do it, I would do it for you, Mustafa,
and your thirteen children, dying of leukemia, in
the hot sun, beside the crumbling well your
father left for you, whose father's father's
father carried the stones, one by one, from
the gold and purple hills to build a garden,
and fountain and courtyard, that are rubble
now, the fig tree you planted for your
children's children poisoned by the same
water irradiated from America, this is too
high a price, my compatriots, is it not, for
our shiny cars, this devil's pact, this dirty
deal for gas, dark karma we are pulling down
on our children's heads, oil fields burning
across the ocean, we should be riding bicycles,
our subways filling up with lethal invisible
smoke

⚸

Kore, the fish daughter, raped again, again,
in the toxic river/shorn wheat field/PCB
riddled ravine behind the concert hall,
what the hell, good for trade, don't you know,
scenic trips to exotic never before seen
underworlds, all this new data, besides, it's
good for character building, a spiritual
exercise, a test, quest, this time Mom's
going for more than a little drought and a
winter tantrum, watch out, Hades, watch out,
the deal she's making with the god Thunder
is not one we want to know, we who once
thought we wanted to know everything,
every daughter and crucified son rising up
out of the blue, black, tumoured, dripping,
these are our bodies, pray for us, this is our
blood

❀

We with wildflowers growing in us,
bittersweet renegade yarrow blossoms
our fathers would have ripped from us,
had they known, but there were wounds
their jealous eyes couldn't see, forest
scenes glittering with unfaithful wives
and hunting knives and poison apples,
this isn't what they wanted, our desperate
queen mothers, long ago they had given
up want, when they turned to leave our
little glass coffins their eyes were blank,
but their arms remembered, and across
these thousand thorns sprung between
us, their bellies ache on starless nights,
for innocent little hands and feet, gasp
against the blue blade, blush of, forgive
us for remembering, unbled unblemished
skin

But don't we all, dear Em, doesn't everyone
have cut off hands gripping knives in their
too big heads, aren't we all blood crazy thirsty
in our midnight selves, to avenge the curdled
mother's milk rotted on our parched cracked
tongues, convinced the death of the little princes
and princesses in the baby tower and the enemy
their king will release us from her untimely
abandonment, like the Pharaoh, like Herod,
like Hitler, like Bush, is this a dagger, divine
Will Shakespeare said, giving the words to
regal Lady Macbeth, I see before me, handle
toward my hand, come, let me clutch thee,
we must be able, he taught us, to imagine at
least this much darkness in us, and then, and
then, Em, then, to wrestle down the spirits
who would delude us into attacking the breathing
world, turning to face the hot fanged wolves
that haunt us, who if we're brave enough,
believe it or not, would rather play, full leafed
trees dancing toward us, the frozen child
huddled asleep, deep in her forest bed shivering
in slow thaw, as we remember ourselves her
father, her mother, and the enemy our sister, brother

※

Cat in high heels, that wasn't the real story,
though her pink painted hind feet and silly
shoes did make a flashy impression, prelude,
foreplay to the real event, you were right,
I was right, to interrupt the tape, right there,
where it made the turn into darkness,
sadistic pleasure,to talk about fear instead,
terror, Inquisition inspired torture at knife
point, terrific haunting across continents,
centuries, all those lives on the outer edge
of the human, calling, shaking, singing,
grieving, coaxing, dancing them, fiercely,
in the face of this new scattering, shattering,
unnecessary stupid tragic war, back in

꙳

She who is us and was slain, and thrown
to the rocks and rain by our own jealous
gods, whose broken flesh is the blood
root of the dying world's infinitely
shimmering green shade, whose slit
heart nourishes every dark worm, has
returned to us, bright feathered and shy,
look! circling the sky around this small
fire we dance her return, she who was
dead is alive, her haunting melodious
cry

꙰

*for Sherry*

One minute you were skimming lightly
through air, the next you were twisted
around your bicycle, your bones learning
the new quantum geometry of angles
without light, only sound, whirling
through dense space to find your way
back to this gravitas, this ground, always
you were the child of lightning, dancing
quickly between clouds, here in your
new arms between sutured elbow and
wrist sings the knowledge of pavement,
of blood that is lust for earth dust, calling
us, calling us down

✳

*for Heidi, at fifty*

You, you were the queen then all afternoon
in the dandelion starred grass, in the royal
rainbow coloured circle skirt from glorious
Tante Jay we struggled over, and you won,
her unfathomable sloe-eyed glamour
imprinted in its mini-pleats like delicious
tantalizing forbidden perfume, I, I was prime
minister in grand swirling black and white,
seducing the villagers with silver tongue
into believing the leftover rags and tatters
were just as nice, see, see here, in the photograph,
everyone is smiling for cake and ice cream,
even nervy Joan, who dared the gods by
marrying our collective grade six village
flame, and lived to design her own grave,
while the rest of us dropped belated children
from our dripping magenta wombs, in another
century he appeared on my city doorstep
with pizza in his hands, her swaying ghost
palpable in the door frame, we, we too,
nibbled at the sexy bruised blue fruit of
the knowledge of mortality, and Helen,
who looks so innocent here, replaced hip
after hip after hip after hip, eventually
becoming more metal than flesh, fondling
the world virtually, her hungry peasant
fingers leaping across the Luddite centuries
into the new noisy asylum in space, everyone
tap dancing madly on our fifty-six allotted
transplanted plastic organ keys

꙰

*after Donna Haraway*

Not ungrateful for the attempt at proper
institutionalization, Mr. Vice President,
these twenty piece place settings inside
your walls, though it is you with your
head in the clouds, engineering our wild
minds with your long armed industrial
screws and custom made hard wired hat,
your poems locked in secret drawers,
invisible you thought, but we have x-ray
eyes, all our night flying has made us
bold, here we come riding quantumly
through your armoured glass windows
on our multicoloured cyborged wings,
still bats, witches, goddesses, still unruly
mistresses of our, your, the world's pulsing
heart

✼

*after Jeffrey Eugenides*

How jealous I was finding your beautiful
morning cock beside me, sister, twin, at fifteen,
carrying your gorgeous difference hidden
beneath girlie skirts all this time, and I the
last to know, no, no, you said, it grew when
my blood and breasts came, no one knows
my secret shame, except Rose Garden Grandma,
who told me in her kitchen at age five, rolling
out sour apple pie dough, I know, I know you,
you're *paeve*, and I didn't know what she meant
until age thirteen, and I feeling only left out
and desirous, O, of the urgent heaviness of
your new maleness and unafraid, though it
frustrated and alarmed you, turned my hungry
woman's body over to cover you, and you
welcomed it, O, that was sweet love we made
that morning, dear twin, you pouring your
urgent flesh into me and my thirsty belly
drinking, drinking, until I knew how to grow
my own, and now walking along the sidewalks
in the electric city I swagger a little, feeling
this sweet naked treasure, do you still have
it too, this masculine softness, this heaviness,
hidden in our jeans

✻

Now I remember, it was you, Grandma,
who swallowed the Wolf, muttering
in your half acre garden and all the time
wild hairy balls dangling under your
skirts, O Grandma, what big, she was
only a little thing, but don't cross her,
rows and rows of juicy green peapods,
slit deftly open by razor Wolf claws,
the better to eat, suckling her youngest,
her favourite, baby, black eyed, sitting
on the carved cherry wood armchair
from the summer kitchen, under the
crooked red crabapple tree, at sundown,
the village boys jostling and shouting
in the grass filled ditches, if only, if only,
he had known his own mother that way,
wet, under the woolly purple hood, so
he wouldn't have had to shake his lonely
stick in the terrified children's faces,
and that one, that one, filled for life with
wrathful apocalyptic fire

✲

Twenty-three years later your death
stabs me, a fresh wound, here I sit
weeping shamelessly live tears for
you, through the window of this prosaic
train, rattling through the cultivated
green fields of southern Ontario, how
surprised you would be, daddy, to know,
who spent your whole life raging for
enough love, how faithful your most
disobedient, angry daughter has been
to you, how truly she carries your belt
marks, your childish joy, your irrational
loyalty to tribe and steppe and wind
and god, how every poet's word, every
quiver of her hungry blood for blast
of prairie sun, and snow, and mouth
on mouth, is inscribed with your grand
beautiful greedy too much peasant
wanting to bend the whole world in
your passionate poetic farmer's hands
love

❋

Nothing in the mauve shadowed silver clods
of evening snow, nothing in the rings of the
bare brown sugar maples lining the frozen river,
nothing in its thick cracked clear February ice,
nothing in the pale orange grey wisped sky,
nothing in the gravel along the side of the road,
nothing in our laminated cross country skis,
nothing in the metal buttons of our down filled
jackets, nothing under our warm tongues, nothing
in the hovering sparrows' beaks, in our snug
bellies, our luminous bones, nothing in our
laughter ringing across the field, nothing in
our plans, our promises, nothing in your wild
eyes, nothing in our grandmother's robust singing
voice we remembered howling with pleasure
this afternoon, nothing in the children's fears,
waking wide eyed in the middle of the night,
nothing in the Kurdish carpet whose rust brown
weave we're so fond of, nothing in the fragrant
steeped peppermint tea on the settee, nothing in
the sparking fire we've lit, the polished apples
we've set out, nothing in this smooth warm brandy,
nothing in our blushing skin, our solid shoulders,
our experienced hands

꙲

*for Anna, in memoriam*

That was the summer we watched the mosquitoes
swarm up from the bushes on the shores of Lake
Winnipeg in great black clouds, against the red
sunset, dense as smoke and humming like out of
control motorcycles, while we stood in awe, half
naked and bareheaded on the sand, protected by
silver winged iridescent blue dragonflies, tiny
angels swooping gracefully around us, while
Ole and Debbie sat in their lawn chairs on the
edge of the water, as they had done for fifty
summers, completely calm, lines perfectly still,
waiting for the pickerel to bite, not saying
whether the scare about the end of the magical
goldeye was city newspaper hype or for real,
that was the summer you left us, coming back
briefly on the fourth evening at midnight, wafting
over the black trees along the Seine River to eat
Montreal bagels and chopped liver from Bernstein's
under the half moon, called to our fire by Gloria's
Anishinabe drum, a ceremony that pleased you,
who reinvented Seder as a gathering of interesting
women discussing experimental films, your spirit
loosening its multicoloured strands, shaking out
courage for us who stayed behind, trailing our
abandoned reservations and villages, you who
thought you didn't know what love was, shining
above us, tenderly, beautiful, lover

# Notes and acknowledgements

'Zone: <le Détroit>' was commissioned by the Art Gallery of Windsor in conjunction with the photographic exhibition by Stan Douglas *Zone: Le Détroit*, curated by Helga Pakasaar, and premiered at the opening in November 1999. Several of the poems were set to music by Paul McIntyre as 'Zone Pomes' and performed by Melinda Enns (soprano) and Paul McIntyre (piano) at the international conference/festival Wider Boundaries of Daring: The Modernist Impulse in Canadian Women's Poetry in October 2001. 'Zone' was published in the *Windsor Review: Transportation*, ed. Dale Jacobs. '5' was published as a broadside for the Mennonite/s Writing conference at Goshen College, Indiana, in 2002.

'Forest slippers' was commissioned by St. Norbert Arts Centre, Winnipeg, as part of the multimedia collaborative project *Language Hotel*, designed by Sheila Butler and curated by Marie Bouchard and Louise Loewen, 2001–2002, and it appeared in the *Language Hotel* CD-ROM and exhibition catalogue, ed. Marie Bouchard, SNAC 2002.

'Wake up' was written in dialogue with Dorothy Livesay's long poem 'Awakening' (Vancouver: Hawthorne Society, 1990) and was set to music by Carol Ann Weaver and Rebecca Campbell. *Awakenings* premiered at the Wider Boundaries of Daring conference at the University of Windsor in October 2001 by Weaver and Campbell, and was recorded on CD with David Travers-Smith in 2003. An excerpt from *Awakenings*, in another format, appeared in *Contemporary Verse 2*.

'Interspecies communication' was commissioned by Aganetha Dyck for a multimedia interspecies installation, *Working in the Dark*, a series of sculpted wax and Braille-inscribed poetic tablets, and premiered at the De Leon White Gallery, Toronto, in 1999. It was co-published as a broadsheet in conjunction with the exhibition and performed at the opening.

'Exhibition notes' remembers *Die Hälfte des Himmels: Chiesische Künstlerinnen der Gegenwart*, curated by Chris Werner and Qin Ping, Frauen Museum, Bonn, Germany, 1999.

'Afterworlds,' 'Castle walk,' 'A modest proposal,' 'St. Norbert in August,' 'St. Norbert in July' and 'Portrait of the artist as a young hero' appeared previously in *Prairie Fire Magazine*. 'Accidentally' appeared in *Canadian Forum*. 'Dog days in Maribor' appeared in *New Quarterly*, with a foreword by Susan Gillis and an afterword by Di Brandt. 'Dreamsongs for Eden' appeared in *Conrad Grebel Review*, with a foreword by Hildi Froese Tiessen. 'Songs for a divorce' appeared in *Six Seasons Review* (South Asia). 'These ways' and 'Now that the secrets' appeared in *River King Poetry Supplement* (us), ed. Glen Sorestad. 'The raw iron taste' and 'If I could end this war' were previously published in *The Common Sky* (Toronto: Three Squares Press, 2003) ed. Stephen Pender, Darren Wershler-Henry and Mark Higgins. 'How jealous I was' and 'The raw iron taste' appeared in the *St. Norbert Arts Centre Newsletter* (January 2003), ed. Doug Melnyk. 'But don't we all, dear Em' appeared in *100 Poets against the War* (Australia: Salt Publishing, 2003), ed. Todd Swift, and was broadcast on CBC Radio.

The René Char citation (p. 7), from 'On the March,' was published in John Thompson's *Collected Poems and Translations*, ed. Peter Sanger (Fredricton, NB: Goose Lane, 1995). Sarain Stump's poem 'He was mixing stars and sand' (p. 11) was published in *Native Poetry in Canada: A Contemporary Anthology* (Calgary, AB: Broadview, 2001), and appeared previously in his collection *There is My People Sleeping* (Sidney, BC: Gray's Publishing, 1970). Steven Michael Berzensky's words (p. 85) are from 'Heart,' which appeared in *Variations on the Birth of Jacob* (Winnipeg: The Muses' Company, 1997). 'Afterworlds' remembers Gwendolyn MacEwen's poetry. The quoted line in 'St. Norbert in August' is from Federico Garcia Lorca, as cited in Erin Moure's *WSW (West South West)* (Montreal: Véhicule, 1989). 'She walks these hills' is from 'Long Black Veil,' by Dylan Wilkin, sung and recorded by Lefty Frizzell in 1959, and later by Big Pink, Johnny Cash, Joan Baez and others. 'Tech Midchuarta' was the name of the beehive-shaped meeting house of the Druids, where they drank sacred honeymead in honour of the queen bee, earthly incarnation of the Queen of Heaven (Philip and Stephanie Carr-Gom, *Druid Animal Oracle*, New York: Simon and Schuster, 1994). 'Feminine monarchie' refers to Charles Butler's 1609 treatise on honeybees, in which he made the controversial claim that the hive was run by women bees, a fact that had apparently been forgotten since ancient times. 'Horizon on fire' hearkens back to René Char's 'The Library on Fire.' 'Misshepezhieu' is the Ojibwa name for the Great Lynx, fierce Guardian Spirit of the Great Lake that is also called Lake Superior.

Thank you to Hawthornden Castle International Writers' Retreat, Scotland; Ledig House International Writers' Retreat, New York; the St. Norbert Arts and Cultural Centre, Winnipeg; Gibraltar Point Centre for the Arts, Toronto; and Le Château de Lavigny, Switzerland, for providing gracious accommodation and stimulating artistic company. I am grateful to the University of Windsor, the Canada Council for the Arts, and External Affairs Canada for generously supporting travel and writing time. Thank you, Martin and Maria Löschnigg, at Karl-Franzens Universität, Graz, Austria, and Michelle Gadpaille and Victor Kennedy at the University of Maribor, Slovenia, for a most hospitable and inspiring guest lectureship in the spring of 2001.

Thanks also to the friends and colleagues whose encouragement sustained me during the writing of these poems, especially Lillian Allen, Bert Almon, Robert Auelletta, Kathy Bergen, Melanie Brannagan, Rebecca Campbell, Margaret Christakos, George Elliott Clarke, Marilyn Dumont, Jenny Erpenbeck, Patrick Friesen, Barbara Godard, Kaiser Haq, Louise Halfe, Heidi and Sara Harms, Ann Hostettler, Alexis Hurtado, Walter Isaac, Fay Lawn, Miram Levine, M. L. Liebler, Daphne Marlatt, Phlip Metres, Philippe Moser, Anna Pellatt, Eunice Scarfe, Jacob Scheier, Sherry Simon, Glen Sorestad, Hildi and Paul Tiessen, Betsy Warland, Carol Ann Weaver, Julia Zacharias and Rachel Zolf. Thank you Jay Millar and Alana Wilcox for excellent editing.

Thank you to my daughters Lisa and Ali, whose energy and imagination keeps stretching mine toward wider horizons, and hugs to Rachel, beloved niece, across these distances.

# About the Author

Di Brandt's award-winning poetry titles include *questions i asked my mother*, *Agnes in the sky* and *Jerusalem, beloved*, for which she received the CAA National Poetry Prize and her second Governor General's Award nomination. She has also published several nonfiction titles, including *Dancing Naked: Narrative Strategies for Writing Across Centuries*. She teaches Creative Writing and Canadian Literature at the University of Windsor. She recently spent a year living and writing in Berlin.

Typeset in Adobe Caslon
Printed and bound at the Coach House on bpNichol Lane, 2003


Cover design based on details from *By the Delta*, a chromogenic
print (36˝ x 72˝) produced collaboratively by Larry Glawson and
Doug Melnyk, 1996, and first presented at the exhibition *Me, me,
me and me*, curated by Sigrid Dahle for the St. Norbert Arts Centre,
running from November 8, 1996, through January 17, 1997.

Coach House Books
401 Huron Street (rear) on bpNichol Lane
Toronto Ontario
M5S 2G5

416 979 2217
1 800 367 6360

mail@chbooks.com
www.chbooks.com